St of FIRE

Andy
Thomas

A Hymn to
Lewes and
the Bonfire
Celebrations

For the people of Lewes

First published in 1999 by S B Publications
19 Grove Road, Seaford, East Sussex, BN25 1TP

© Copyright Andy Thomas 1999

Photographs by Andy Thomas (1998)
Video images by Eve Branston (past years)
Pope & tableau (1998) on pages 41 & 42 courtesy of *Sussex Express*
Image editing by Jason Porthouse

ISBN 1 85770 193 3

Other books by Andy Thomas:

Fields Of Mystery
Quest For Contact (with Paul Bura)
Vital Signs

Typeset and printed by
The Adland Print Group Ltd.
Unit 11, Bellingham Trading Estate,
Franthorne Way, London SE6 3BX.
Tel: 0181 695 6262 Fax: 0181 695 6300

Contents

Front cover watercolour by Siân Wilkins

Acknowledgments

Several people have given indispensible help in the preparation of this book and I wish to express alphabetical gratitude to the following...

Steve Benz for once again placing his faith in me; *Rodney Castleden* for helpful information; *Caroline Dorling* of Flint House for access to her window ledge (!); *Phil Flowers* for encouragement and advice; *Mark Hewitt* for telephone numbers and character references; *Jenny Keen* for being my partner-in-crime on the Fifth and, most of all, for being a special friend over the years; *Martin Noakes* for the use of his colour printer; *Barry Reynolds* for the *attempted* use of his colour printer; *Mum and Dad Thomas* for instilling in me a love of fireworks and Bonfire Night; *David Swingland* for computer advice.

And very special alphabetical thanks to these good people...

John Bleach for opening my eyes to the concept of Lewes as a ritual mound complex, allowing me to use this information and for vetting my historical details (see also Appendix for references to his work); *Eve Branston* for the kind use of her video images; *Andy Freeman* for checking the text from a Bonfire Society perspective, proofing, and for his generous foreword; *Andy Gammon* for the use of his dramatic painting and allowing me to climb Brack Mount; *Jason Porthouse* for photo editing, digital screen grabs and artistic advice; *Kaye Thomas*, as always, for proofing and encouragement during the writing process, ever a treasure; *David Russell* for help with the Lewes map; *Siân Wilkins* for making sense of my ideas for her beautiful cover painting.

My deepest appreciation.

Foreword

by ANDY FREEMAN
Chairman of Cliffe Bonfire Society

FOR those of us hopelessly infected with the Bonfire bug it sometimes comes as a surprise to discover that among our friends, relations and colleagues there are those for whom the Fifth is a one night a year event - albeit just as enjoyable.

While Lewes Bonfire Boys and Girls proudly profess that the celebrations would take place with nobody on the streets to witness their passing, an early evening topic of conversation will invariably be just how busy it is around the War Memorial or how many deep the crowd is on Cliffe Bridge. The challenge of threading the intricate and complicated series of fiery processions through the crowded ancient streets provides a perverse form of pleasure for the captains and officers of the various societies whose skills leave the unaware agog and control-hungry authorities in these over-regulated times exasperated.

As a youngster with an insatiable appetite for Bonfire I discovered Arthur Beckett's book *The Spirit of the Downs* with its brace of stirring chapters about the history of our celebrations and an observer's view of pre-World War One festivities. Despite the passing of nearly a century, the excitement and drama of Lewes on the Fifth still burst from its pages and many times I have returned to Beckett's words for inspiration.

Andy Thomas is one of those odd people with whom I associate (whom it must be said are in the majority!) who doesn't have Bonfire in his blood, but does have Lewes running through his veins. Before reading his book I was surprised to learn that he hadn't discovered *Spirit* and then struck by the similarity of this contemporary observer's view of Bonfire with that of Beckett's.

I read *Streets of Fire* on a leisurely train journey to the

West Country and as we trundled through the rolling hills of Devon and into the home of the county's famous barrel burners, I suddenly experienced an overwhelming sense of home-sickness and an urge to return to this cradle of the Downs. Andy has captured the spirit of Bonfire, but more than this has also managed to capture the very essence of Lewes that makes those who stray eager to return and those who arrive determined never to leave.

Something in Lewes, whether it be deep within its people or even deeper in its history, provokes an independence of thought and a determination to turn thought into deed. Bonfire provides that outlet. Long may it and the people who enjoy it so much, be they participant or spectator, continue.

ANDY FREEMAN
May 1999

Remember, remember the Fifth of November
The Gunpowder Treason and plot
I see no reason why Gunpowder Treason
Should ever be forgot

Guy Fawkes, Guy Fawkes 'twas his intent
To blow up the King and the Parliament
Three score barrels of powder below
Poor old England to overthrow

By God's providence he was catch'd
With a dark lantern and burning match
Holler boys, holler boys, ring bells ring
Holler boys, holler boys, God Save the King!

A penny loaf to feed old Pope
A farthing cheese to choke him
A pint of beer to rinse it down
A faggot of sticks to burn him

Burn him in a tub of tar
Burn him like a blazing star
Burn his body from his head
Then we'll say old Pope is dead

Hip Hip Hoorah!
Hip Hip Hoorah!
Hip Hip Hoorah!

Traditional

Introduction

There's a line in Woody Allen's classic film *Manhattan* which runs: *"He adored New York City... he romanticised it out of all proportion... New York was his town and it always would be."*

These are very much my feelings for Lewes. I was born in this town and have lived in or around it my whole life. After all these years I still get excited at walking its attractive streets, admiring its scenic beauty, exploring its inspiring topography and soaking up the unique energy it seems to generate. There's something magical here. If I do romanticise it a little, I'm not alone in this.

Lewes sits on the arm of a soft hill just a few miles from the south east coast of England, stretching down to a river valley surrounded by a large irregular bowl of East Sussex downland. An estuary around 2000 years ago, the waters have receded leaving only marshlands and the Ouse as their legacy. The county town of Sussex for many years, Lewes has seen the eye of commerce fluctuate through changes of industry and economic climates, but remains a thriving community in picturesque surroundings, the impression given to most passing through.

But Lewes has facets not so immediately obvious to casual visitors and a history which belies its apparently calm surface. Both the wounds of past events and the joy of ritual and tradition run strong here and never is this more conspicuous than on November the Fifth. For one night of the year, Lewes suddenly explodes into ceremony, celebration and commemoration; a vast pageant of fire takes place which invades the streets - to the continuing alarm of authorities - with flaming torch processions, the burning of controversial effigies, the practice of strange customs and five simultaneous firework displays. This is far more than a frivolous festivity. On the Fifth, past ages of religious upheaval, persecution and war are brought to the surface for remembrance and Bonfire, as the night has become known, attempts to strike a blow for public freedom of expression in a way lost or denied to most communities today.

Sometimes known as Guy Fawkes night, this celebration has long been marked around the British Isles each November the Fifth with fire and pyrotechnics, but as the final days of the 20th century draw to a close, it is a tradition which is dying. Although municipal firework displays continue as a pale remnant in some districts, others have fallen dark in recent years, happy to allow antiquated ways from a long forgotten time to fade.

Yet one or two places steadfastly - almost stubbornly - refuse to let go. Ottery St Mary in Devon is one last such impressive example but nowhere is Bonfire adhered to more strongly and on such a scale as Lewes.

The first steps towards the events honoured on the Fifth began with King Henry VIII's messy rejection of what he saw as tyrannical Papal interference in the affairs of another country. With the subsequent 'Reformation' in the 1530s, which would lead in time to the foundation of today's Church of England, British history underwent a turbulent period of religious subjugation and bloody strife through incoming monarchs' shifting denominational loyalties. The 17 Protestant martyrs burnt at Lewes between 1555 and 1557 during the country's brief return to Catholicism under Queen Mary were, sadly, just small examples of the hatred and murder stirred.

Thus, as Protestants again returned to power, when a Roman Catholic conspiracy against King James I was uncovered in 1605 and the unfortunate figure of Guy Fawkes was caught guarding barrels of gunpowder intended to blow up the House of Lords and the King with it, an official Act was passed that this deliverance from the evils of Papist oppression should be remembered forever. Thereafter, by law, each November the Fifth the anniversary of the Gunpowder Plot's fall was marked accordingly with fires and bell-ringing, primarily as an encitement to fuel Catholic persecution. Yet for the people at large it quickly began to absorb elements from existing fire festivals with far deeper roots...

As years went by, different governments and monarchs would attempt to use Bonfire for their own politically manipulative ends but, ironically, began to fear and suppress the steadily anarchic mode of observance which was starting to express itself in riotous unrest. For all the religious undertones, Bonfire slowly became a more general declaration of freedom of thought. Despite its original intention as a reaffirmation of *authority*, liberation is what it came to represent and never more so than in Lewes.

Although the strength of the celebrations waxed and

waned over the centuries, Lewes obstinately continued to obey the original Act and has held dear a strange mixture of the old and new principles of Bonfire. Its practice in the town has been a long struggle against official orders banning it in times of feared revolution and attempts to water down its more rowdy elements. The gangs of 'Bonfire Boys' dressed as Guernsey-shirted striped smugglers (though other costumes of disguise developed), who formed to protect the tradition, in time developed into the less militant but no less resolute 'Bonfire Societies' which organise the events of today. Six remain in existence, named after local districts; Cliffe, Commercial Square, Lewes Borough, Nevill Juvenile, South Street and Waterloo. Each arranges events throughout the year and mounts the processions and displays of the Fifth (although Nevill holds its main observance the week before). They come together just once for the backbone of the evening, the Grand Procession, with the historical exception of Cliffe and, in more recent years, South Street, both of which maintain independence. Though the societies' social activities of fund-raising, charitable events and fancy dress competitions may seem happily innocuous to the nonchalant observer, a heart of fiery dedication and protectiveness beats still.

It's here, then, that it must be decreed what this book is *not* about. It is NOT a history of the Gunpowder Plot, nor is it even the story of Bonfire in Lewes over the years, although its background plays a role. I am not a Bonfire Society member and don't presume to speak for them. Their story has been well-documented elsewhere by those far more qualified and references to such works are given in the Appendix. This book is written resolutely from a *spectator's* point of view - an under-explored yet vital part of the Fifth, however much outsiders are now being discouraged from attending due to crowd problems, a tension as yet unresolved.

So what *is Streets of Fire* about? Bonfire in Lewes is the

visible output of many enduring threads and influences with origins transcending the obvious, going back even before the Gunpowder Plot and shaped not only by events but perhaps by the town's very location, as the closing Epilogue explores. Bonfire is the expression of an entire people and captures and distils the spirit of a community like no other manifestation. For all the excellent histories, press reports and examinations available, few have captured the true force of what it is to experience Bonfire in Lewes *today* and what the night has to say about its inhabitants. Even fewer have described the celebrations from a Lewesian onlooker's perspective, who has the opportunity to interact with the proceedings in a broader way denied to a Society member tied to their own events.

Taking one November the Fifth, this book roams through the streets of Lewes to experience as many events of a Bonfire night as possible in an attempt to capture its real magic, moods, humour and essence, the fine but crucial details which make it what it is. Rather than a dry documentary, it is composed as a very personal view and is impressionistic - and indeed romanticised - rather than journalistic, seen through my eyes, but eyes which I hope will reflect the experience of many. Likewise, some of the accompanying photographs, uncaptioned and interwoven with the text, are abstract and dreamlike rather than picture postcards, placed mostly with chronological logic but occasionally plucked out of order as befits. The chronology itself, as marked by times preceding each titled section, is sequential but fittingly loose for an evening which rarely runs to the dot.

As a personal recording, it is clearly impossible to be in all places at once and as such this document of my travels through the streets may leave one or two stones unturned, some societies' activities better highlighted than others. But there is no agenda of bias in this, simply the inevitability of its perspective. All the major events are present.

Throughout this telling, using asides and observations, I

try to convey something of what it is to be a true Lewesian, reaching to find just why the traditions of Bonfire burn so bright here. As intimated above, there is growing evidence to show that, whatever else it has become, it may be an echo from a much deeper past; noted before by others but still little recognised. Some may find a few of the reasons given for this in the Epilogue controversial, but if it inspires discussion something will have been achieved. At the very least, I hope to invite the curious to look again at the little explored origins of specific aspects of the Lewes landscape, seeing their implications in a new light.

As for Lewes itself, another thing this book *isn't* is a history of the town. But knowing a little of its background will help put things into context.

From the start of its inhabited life the protection fostered by Lewes's somewhat enclosed location seemed to encourage a more distinctive and independent development from outside populations, seeping into the culture and personalities of its people. There is a basic, straight-talking quality to Lewesians that can seem brusque to newcomers, born perhaps of an eternal suspicion of the outside world and of any newfangled ideas which might threaten the ordered balance of local life. Won over, they can be fiercely loyal and protective and their good humour and strong community spirit is revealed. It is telling that Sussex was the final region of England to be converted to Christianity; it resisted imposed change to the last, a trait especially fierce in Lewes. Yet once accepted, the sanctity of the new religion in the two imposed forms it would take was fanatically defended to the hilt, as Bonfire itself clearly illustrates.

The Anglo-Saxons, who effectively set up what would become the Lewes we know today, built their first settlements along an arm of downland promontory sweeping headlong from Blackcap, eventually to become the line of the High Street. The districts of Cliffe and Southover developed as distinctly separate villages before being absorbed in later centuries. The arrival of the Normans saw the creation of Lewes's crowning structure, the castle, unusually constructed *within* the surrounding town walls, perhaps because of the usefulness of its site. Built to spy and repel invaders from its major vantage point with clear vistas on all sides, the towering presence also reminded the local inhabitants of just who was in charge. From this point, Lewes grew up as defensive town - in more ways than one - and building shaped itself around the fortress. Walls came and went, boundaries changed and slowly the town grew.

That Lewes so prides itself each November the Fifth on remembering the saving of King and Parliament may in part be due to the formative battle of 1264 which took place on the high fields which swept down from what is now Nevill (although its exact location is disputed). When Simon de Montfort led the might of the English barons' forces against the reigning King Henry III, the subsequent agreement with the defeated monarch would eventually mould the creation of the democracy we know today. Unfortunately, over a thousand men reputedly died to achieve it; more blood on Lewes' historical hands. Perhaps this explains why, almost four hundred years later, Lewes kept its head down during the English Civil war as a general Parliamentary stronghold and curtailed its involvement. It had shouldered its fill of conflict. The Reformation in 1537 had already destroyed its most holy place at the hands of Henry VIII's anti-Papal forces, the huge priory at Southover reduced to ruins, and Queen Mary's vengeance as the needle swung momentarily against Protestantism had made smoking ruins of 17 human beings. Little wonder the struggle against oppression would be so remembered here.

Despite the general Protestant bias which finally set in, disillusionment with both Christian churches made Lewes a hotbed of religious non-conformity in later years. The high profile of Quakers and other heretical sects in the community bred yet more persecution, if rather less lethal than before. The fleeing of religious refugees to America led to Lewes having strong links with the 'New World' and once again the town helped shape the future world order; Thomas Paine, an outspoken, opinionated individual who upset many an Englishman with his radical views in the late 1700s, lived here for a few years before heading off across the Atlantic where his book *Common Sense* would help inspire the American War of Independence. *"I still pursue, and ever will, the same path... the path of liberty,"* he once wrote.

These words could describe the mindset of Lewes over the centuries. Despite the gorier chapters of its past, it has always come out fighting once more for liberty. Yet a kind of English conservatism always prevented outright revolution. Maybe because of its troubled history the expression of Lewesians' views through funnelled, controlled valves like that of Bonfire replaced direct confrontation.

Religious antagonism in the town is virtually extinct today and has been much exaggerated by those stirring cheap shocks and the media seeking an 'angle'. Though the trappings of religious intolerance remain in the traditions of Bonfire, with its anti-Papist banners, things have moved on, as this book hopes to show, to represent something wider, more liberating.

I hope *Streets of Fire* will stand as a valuable testament to the spirit of contemporary Lewes whilst recalling what it has been and act as a time capsule for anyone coming across a brown and crumbling remain of this book in the far future, of something special which, as the rhyme dictates, deserves to be remembered.

ANDY THOMAS

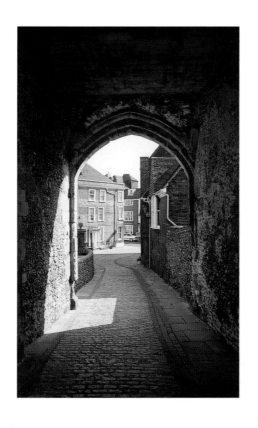

The Preceding Weeks

The spirit of Bonfire grows quietly long before the Fifth. As a child, fireworks were an endless fascination for me, colourful and alive, beings in their own right which enjoyed a short but spectacular life. My two sisters and I would watch for them from our window across the Winterbourne estate as the late weeks of October drew on and local families began to have bonfire parties. A wall of houses stretched out, rising to Lewes prison, an unlikely landmark terminating the skyline. And just occasionally, from between the rooftops, a silver or golden streak would suddenly illuminate the tiles or a distant pop would have us turning in all directions for the source. You had to be sharp or you would only just catch the last fading sparks. A common wind-up for the three of us would be to *say* that we'd just seen a rocket everyone else had missed, adding a little vocal sound effect behind the hand if really desperate.

This waiting game would be played almost every evening as the Fifth approached, heads under the curtains, lights off. The very rareness of sightings somehow made each success more magical, though faint echoing bangs and crashes would begin to grow in frequency as October waned. The expectation was almost unbearable, pacified a little by the arrival of the large brown paper bag with the protruding sticks which signified the buying of the family fireworks. We would be allowed, in daily rations, to look at these wonderful, brightly-coloured little packages of gunpowder which rattled when you shook them (to parental protest). How could such pretty sparkles and fierce explosions be held in such small, friendly-looking containers? Their *potential* was the most exciting thing, the thought that for a few seconds only they would come alive and dance on the appointed night. The reading of Oscar Wilde's *The Remarkable Rocket* only confirmed to my infant mind that each decorated tube had a personality of its own and as such fireworks were treated with love and respect in our house.

Of course, back then I had no concept of the months of preparation going on all around to prime Lewes for celebrations on a scale of which I was entirely unaware and wouldn't be until my growing years enabled later nights and more adventures. Preliminary Society displays out in the provinces, secret tableaux being designed and built, procession routes planned and verified, huge bonfires being constructed at different sites across the town, official badges being collected the night before... All this was unknown to me. Bonfire was a mystical occurrence which just *happened* and the costumed players on street corners or those who knocked on the door after tea selling programmes were just another part of that mystery. Even for many adult spectators today it is taken as given that the incredible proceedings will simply *be there.*

The slog of the societies to mount and maintain the traditions is one which may never be fully appreciated by those on the other side of the crowd barriers. But the reward for the organisers and costumed marchers is the experience itself. Eyes that look on are simply a side-effect, tolerated but not necessarily encouraged by those exercising their claim to the freedom of the streets. Paradoxically, this adds yet another crucial edge to the Fifth in Lewes; it's not just the Bonfire Boys who tread a slightly subversive course. One's very presence as a spectator is a small act of defiance against those who would be happier not to see the thousands of onlookers there at all.

The Fifth

10:17hrs   Expectation

There's already an air of anticipation and shoppers seem to move just a little faster than usual, with a kind of agitated wariness. The Fifth has already officially begun with the launching of a large maroon at daybreak. An eve-of-

Armageddon atmosphere pervades the streets as if civilisation is preparing to brace itself against some unspecified disaster. Workmen with large planks and wooden crates appear and begin to cover the windows of individual shops, although for some protection has mysteriously arrived overnight. It's always curious to see which traders are prepared to brave the risks of vandals or body crush on glass and neglect precautions. Few at major gathering spots take a chance, like those around the War Memorial which will play such a pivotal role this evening at the centre of the town. Printed cards or scribbles displayed in shop fronts invariably warn of early closing today, as some plan to evacuate, batten down for siege or take to the streets to join in with plenty of time to spare.

Dawn also seems to have risen on the unseen materialisation of metal torch drums and flapping banners placed at strategic points throughout the streets. For one day only, Cliffe High Street has become a bastion of anti-Catholicism - of a historical rather than contemporary kind - as the ominous NO POPERY slogan looms and another flag remembers the long-deceased but not forgotten Protestant martyrs burnt so

many centuries ago further up the town. Oddly, overlooking the actual site of that morbid echo from the past, another banner shouts SUCCESS TO WATERLOO near the Town Hall while others make their mark elsewhere.

This year (1998), sinister Orwellian bell-like public address speakers quietly appear on roof ledges and lamp posts. From these will be barked orders from the new herding regime enforced on spectators tonight by the police, enraging those conducting solemn rituals at the stone monument.

 Adding to the air of control, large lorries begin to draw up, stacked high with gun-metal crowd barrier gratings, later secured in the gutters at strategic spots, more than usual this Fifth. Litter bins are then removed for safety onto council vans - one liberty which *will* be granted today is the license to drop refuse into the road, to join the detritus of charred torch-wood soon to be piling up. The air of expectancy builds.

16:33   Gatherings

The last shops are closing up now, road blocks are appearing on the outskirts of the town and there's a notable increase of striped jerseys strolling with intent to their respective Society headquarters on designated street corners of tradition. The sky is darkening and the November air notably cooling. Clear, cold nights seem the archetypal Bonfire Night conditions which nature provides - but sometimes it pulls dirty tricks. The year before will always be remembered as one such prank, in which pounding rain saw to it that every nook, crevice and chink in  clothing and flesh, be it anoraked or costumed, was saturated sooner or later. Even waterproofs seemed to give in after a while as crawling rivulets performed Trojan invasions. But not this year. Mist and clouds threaten for a while but do nothing but block the stars.

Already squealing rockets are lighting up the sky with increasing frequency and barely a minute goes by without the crump of an 'air-bomb' or 'rookie' (rook-scarer) making itself known somewhere in the Lewes air. This is the beginning of a continual torrent of minor and major explosions which will build from a combination of Society members' japes, family firework parties and rowdy street louts, peak with the monumental crescendo of the *five* separate organised displays and tail off only as the small hours approach.

17:37   Movement

The sounds of marching bands are beginning to drift across Lewes and on the breeze to the surrounding villages. It's amazing how far away they can be heard. The first processions are taking place, each Society marking out ritual territory with a series of highly specific marches which will run throughout the evening. There's an almost ethereal quality to the music echoing deceptively through the streets; wandering around trying to find its source can be confusing, a kind of surreal game where just when you think you're heading in the right direction for spectacle, another band seems to start up behind and the search begins again. Soon, however, you can't fail to come across one of the many processions which play such a large part of this deep tradition, flaming torches radiating the air. Caught in some of the narrower residential roads, you can find yourself almost pressed against the walls as facial protection from the glow. Families gather in open doorways, the chattering sound of the evening news within soon drowned by brass and drum. A few doors remain stubbornly shut, curtains drawn. One can only assume those who elect to leave their cars in marchers' paths don't mind hazarding charred and scratched paintwork once a year.

For one night only, vehicular movement is barred and the liberation of the streets allowed, albeit reluctantly. Once, the struggle to maintain this right to express open defiance of those who would oppress was a violent and dangerous affair. The struggle has been streamlined and tamed by necessary allowances on the part of local authorities, but you can tell the fear of such expression remains. For the first time, side roads and passageways (or 'twittens'), the arteries to the High Street, have been blocked this year,

 restricting pedestrian access to strictly controlled zones. A friend even finds himself turned away from entering the road of his own home and told to go the long way around. This is only liberation of a kind then. Somebody's afraid of something. Count the policemen lining the streets. Who or what are they protecting in such large numbers?

As the first marches proceed, not all take to the streets so early. Families with children are being fed and watered early to bolster them against the cold air which awaits. For many, the evening will begin with the Grand United Procession when many of the disparate marches come together for the one and only time. Jacket potatoes, sausages and grated cheese, of course, remain the traditional Bonfire fare, either following or preceding fireworks in the garden, where those little coloured packages come to life at last.

18:07   Tar

Already the pavements are filling with people and picturesque Cliffe Bridge is the scene.

One practice which scared authorities in centuries past was the perilous rolling of flaming tar barrels through the streets. One can only imagine the spectacular chaos of a fireball careering down the steep slopes of School Hill (from the War Memorial to Cliffe). These days, 'streamlining' and safety regulations have developed the art into Cliffe's tamer but hardly risk-free 'tar barrel' race. Dissected oil drums filled with burning debris and mounted on carts are

pulled at great speed along Cliffe High Street to the bridge by the ladies and then returned to Cliffe Corner by the men. They wait at the arched summit above the Ouse, Guernsey-shirted Bonfire Boys gripping the drag handles with all the intense concentration of any sportsman

awaiting a gun. The crowds spilling into the road are cajoled back again by Society members and police (in this case, justifiably). No-one will want to be in the way of these flaming projectiles.

Tension for the start grows. Old hands know the routine but novices expecting a simple shout of "Go!" don't know Lewes Bonfire. A deep thunderclap-like boom which knocks the eardrums an inch or so into the brain and reverberates the

bowels suddenly leaps tourists out of their skin as the race begins. The speed of the participants is so great they are almost out of sight before you've noticed them go by, a streaking trail of fire receding up the street to cheers.

18:24   Remembrance

The most solemn focus of the Fifth has already begun. The War Memorial, a stone needle adorned by gargantuan pre-Raphaelite angels, is visited by each major Society in turn. Over the next hour or so wreaths are placed, silences held, the Last Post played. This is where one begins to touch the

heart of Lewes Bonfire. Once the aroma of burning martyrs
wafted sickeningly across this square from outside the old

Star Inn, now the Town Hall. It has
not been forgotten. No mere carnival
or mindless frivolity, tonight victims
are remembered; victims of persecution,
victims of oppression, and here,
victims of
war. Firework
poppies make
the point.
The epitaph

LEST WE FORGET blazes quietly.
The High Street momentarily falls
silent from rookies and raised voices.

The square around the monument is packed with onlookers.
Surrounding windows and ledges are filled with human
silhouettes, precariously balanced partly for a view but

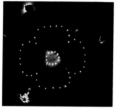

mostly to edge closer to these
special moments.

The Tannoys crackle into life. The
police have decided to make a
routine announcement, the same as
every other one irritatingly transmitted
across the streets tonight from the

sinister horns: Stay on the pavement. Don't do this. Don't
do that. Now is not the time for such messages and anger

at the broken sacred silence
will spill over into the
'sermon' at Commercial
Square's Bonfire Prayers a
few hours later and pages of
the local newspaper the following week. Fluorescent-
coated officers have already

been preventing people from making their way up School
Hill for the commemoration despite plentiful gaps among

the crowds. Protests unheeded, a block of people clog the halfway point of the hill but I manage to slip by in a moment of lapsed vigilance.

The fluorescent coats are at least less provocative than the riot gear and batons worn one recent year, stirring a storm of subsequent protest. Such distrust of the public and sheer misunderstanding of the spirit of Bonfire *made* you feel riotous at the sight. On this, at least, someone realised a

mark had been over-stepped and shields and visors were dropped or at least kept well hidden from thereon. That such measures were thought (wrongly) necessary for even one year is at least an

illustration of the power of Lewes Bonfire. Who can remember any real trouble breaking out in recent years? The proceedings have already become a form of very controlled anarchy. Clearly some are not convinced it is controlled enough. Not that every officer is a faceless robot; some smile, show courtesy and even dare to display enjoyment at the celebrations. This must be encouraged for the future. Fear is not the way forward.

18:55   Ouse

By now, crowds are gathering again at Cliffe Bridge, where a number of societies stop off to cast a burning tar barrel into the waters of the Ouse. With so many heaving bodies and bobbing heads struggling to catch this sight, it's hard to see exactly what's going on and when the moment comes it's over in a flash of sparks and a sizzle as the barrel plunges from the railings into the murky depths. Like a number of Bonfire traditions, few remember how this particular ritual came about (something about old Society boundary squabbles) but it's there all the same and must, like everything else this evening, be maintained at all costs.

19:34   Commemoration

As part of the territory marking, societies process several times to a given stop-off in cyclic loops, and Cliffe Bridge is a pivotal station. On returning from the wreath-laying, Cliffe rendezvous here yet again and ignite a small effigy

of the Martyrs' Memorial, another stone needle which gazes out from Cuilfail hill, lit up just this one night of the year, visible from the whole town as a reminder to the inhabitants of Lewes of its sadder legacy. *Land of Hope and Glory* plays as the 17 victims of historical stupidity and intolerance, named on the banner twisted by the wind, are remembered. Some see the traditional Protestant bias and No Popery antics of some of the societies as a form of paradoxical intolerance in itself but 'traditional' is the key word here. If Guy Fawkes had been Protestant and King James I Catholic no doubt things would simply be reversed.   Bonfire ploughs a wider

agenda now, of striking a general blow for freedom of thought. There's little evidence of any religious hatred in the eyes of the people who carry the traditions today and those who attempt to stir it are by and large outsiders to the town or journalists

seeking sensation. Catholic clergy occasionally trigger fresh controversy by speaking out against what they see as a threat to their beliefs yet the truth is that no-one but the odd extremist (who one may find on any side) seems remotely interested in preventing the practice of faith. Though my world-view has moved on since, I was brought up a Catholic in Lewes and no-one ever harassed me.

But those attempting to follow the procession down from the War Memorial to witness the martyrs' remembrance find themselves having to strike a blow for their own liberation this year. Despite Eastgate Street being clear of marchers, who simply cross from School Hill into Cliffe, the police aren't allowing anyone across, creating a dangerous plug of people piling up at the foot of the hill. People are protesting but set-jawed officers aren't budging. Again, only subterfuge finally enables me and my companion to make a break for it when their  attention is briefly diverted but by then the martyrs' tableau has expired and we're too late. So much for freedom of the streets.

19:35   Party

Aside from High Street remembrances, in many homes families are now hastily discharging their own fireworks, one eye on the clock, before heading out to the Grand Procession. This was always a enchanting time for me as a child. By now that unique all-pervading hint of smoke which can only mean it's Bonfire Night is in the air. Any other time it might be an irritant, but the blanket of light smog which descends over the town tonight is an essential part of the atmosphere. Where else in the world do so many firework parties break out all at once? You can spend as much time watching the emanations of coloured fire from neighbouring gardens as your own. It's a communal thing and if a rocket goes off with a particularly loud bang cheers can often be heard from several streets around. This is the one night people don't mind having money to burn.

And fair amounts of money must ignite in certain households judging by the quality and length of some mini-displays.

Although nothing can compete with the major exhibitions which will be bombarding Lewes in just a couple of hours, there's something special about spending an intimate moment with one little tube throwing out sparkly fragments for a few precious seconds. Lost to the collective in large co-ordinated discharges, at home each little dance, twist and glow is appreciated on a different but equally valid scale. And if a rocket decides to go awry and blow up next door's hedge, well, that's just an added bonus.

There are some who would end these simple pleasures. Each year we hear of more threatened legislation against the public purchase of fireworks - even the societies have found their hands increasingly bound by ever-tightening safety regulations which make no allowance for the special case of Lewes. There are always tragedies, of course, and who could not feel sympathy for those innocently hurt by these deceptively pretty looking bombs? But many accidents are caused by open misuse. It would be a tragedy of its own if the small joy of garden fireworks were removed or reduced to pathetic sparks.

But we loved them. How many Catholics are really anti-Bonfire in Lewes? My family certainly weren't. In the early 1970s even our parish priest would join us with other friends to help celebrate our humble display. Whether, in a classic family legend, he felt this was such a good idea after a Jumping Jack once leapt into his wellington, making him, in turn, jump across the garden before throwing off the offending boot, isn't recorded. (Perhaps understandably in this case, Jumping Jacks were among the first fireworks to meet the legislative axe.)

As the last cracker died we would always cut the time schedule too fine and suddenly find ourselves rushing to put extra layers on and fighting relatives for lavatory time (no small matter - the Fifth can be a long evening with few facilities in this department) before careering out of the house and dashing up Rotten Row for 'The Grand'. Nine times out of ten the procession would be late and we'd find ourselves exhausted and puffing for nothing.

20:01   Procession

Waiting anywhere along the length of the town's main artery gives one of the most dramatic insights into the

commitment and soul of this extraordinary night. We always used to stand opposite Shelleys Hotel at the western end of the High Street. Here the land rises up the promontory Lewes is built on and gives a spectacular view of the march coming down but each has their own favourite prime position.

Just watching other spectators pouring down the hill ahead of the Grand, trying to find a place to settle, is an insight in itself. Tonight, thousands upon thousands have streamed into town on specially scheduled trains or buses, or parked their cars on the outskirts which usually resemble the Gulf War's road to Basra, vehicles pulled over onto any available ground at all sorts of angles, trailing out as far as the outlying roundabouts. If authorities wanted to be really nasty, they could make a killing in parking fines, but, for one night only, a blind eye is turned. The huge influx of visitors is a dilemma for the Bonfire societies who have recently begun to actively discourage outsiders from flocking in, partly for reasons of security and cost, but also through patriotism. A victim of its own success, Bonfire was never developed as a spectator sport but as a heartfelt statement of its inhabitants, who now find themselves hemmed in each Fifth by immigrants from the outside world. The town has come to question the presence of those here to gawp. Even an ingenious Bonfire radio station set up especially this year openly *dissuades* the masses from attending. Yet the fascination is undeniable, the draw of this incredible spectacle hard to resist. It is a quandary which remains.

All peoples are here, whether outsider or Lewesian. Old, young (in some cases too young - is this really the place for babies, with flames and rookies never far away?), able, disabled, with all classes represented. Some stand politely, waiting quietly, others bawdier, not least the inevitable yobs who roam, drunken and foul-mouthed, inspiring the thought that maybe Neanderthal Man didn't die out after all. (In fairness, Bonfire history seems to suggest this element was rather *more* prevalent in the old violent days of its expression.) Street vendors wander by selling those peculiar but attractive glowing necklaces and other sparkly trinkets you only seem to see on the Fifth, eager to catch the attention of kids, all-too-easily hooked by the charm of their wares, forcing parental surrender. I remember one such necklace breaking on a person next to me at a display a few years back. I was splattered like a starscape by a frighteningly luminous liquid which, rumour suggests, employs a very low level radioactive sub-stance. After initial fears, I didn't die of radiation poisoning.

A van with loudspeakers suddenly appears at the brow of Western Road, alongside St Pancras Catholic church, my old spiritual base, which lies low, lights doused. Even at the end of the 19th century, some intolerance did remain and heavy protests greeted the construction of this, the first Roman Catholic church in Lewes since the Reformation, which destroyed the huge priory of the same name at Southover. But here is evidence that things *have* changed and that tradition, not modern bigotry, is the watchword now - no-one bats an eyelid as the first ranks of torch bearers pass by.

Echoes of a mutated-beyond-understanding amplified voice float through the street, apparently asking people to clear the road, underpinned by the first, but unmistakable strains of a brass band, drums thundering distantly. This time, there is no doubt which direction it's going to be coming in. The first flicker of blazing torches bobs into view and the head of a procession which can take over half an hour to pass by is suddenly with you.

There's a curious mirror to this event each Good Friday, taking the same initial course, in which many of the Christian denominations of Lewes gather to prove their new unity and tolerance. Instead of flaming torches, a large wooden cross is solemnly carried through the High Street from St Pancras church to the mysterious and possibly ancient mound (or 'Tump') at Mountfield Road, where it is erected as if to Christianise what might be a pagan site. It's an atmospheric and beautiful event. But as hymns are sung and the last golden glow of the setting sun illuminates the cruciform reminder of the most famous martyr without whom  Bonfire would not exist as we know it, I can never help sensing the glimmer of an important but elusive connection beyond the obvious, between the unexplained mound, the marchers and the cross, and the Guy Fawkes celebrations. This notion will be brought into sharper focus for me atop Chapel Hill the following morning of this very Fifth.

Tonight though, the Grand Procession is full of colour and noise, and the crosses carried are burning ones. Others bear large flaming keys amongst other symbols, the key to the freedom of the streets. Societies from all around the county have come together to join their Lewes cousins to produce this massive and breathtaking scene, minus Cliffe and South Street, who prefer to tread their own paths. Integrated with the inevitable striped Guernseys, elaborate costumes, the legacy of painstaking summer hours of construction or grooming, are paraded; Red Indians with long trailing feathers, Cromwellian soldiers, sequinned Valencians, Tudor ladies, Zulu warriors with neck-breakingly high head-dresses... And, of course, ecclesiastical dress is to the fore as members of the mock clergy who will lead the assault on the effigies hoisted high above the throng lead their 'flock'. All humanity from many cultures

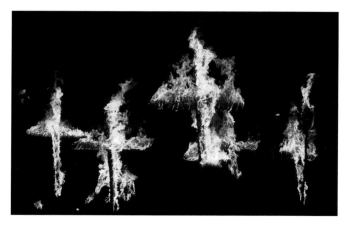

and eras seems to be represented somewhere, the choice of costume descending from long traditions, the meanings, some born of past events or political protests, now obscured by time. More comedic touches also appear; clowns, alluring wild schoolgirls escaped from St Trinian's, wacky outfits of various persuasions...

But the light touch of some simple local carnival is missing, replaced with something deeper. Rather than the uniformly smiling, carefree faces one might expect, many have a look of grim determination in the eyes. Nearly all bear torches of flame, carefully bound fabric dipped in flammable liquid and held on thin wooden stakes, the fire reminding people

of the greater purpose which brought these proceedings into existence. There's enjoyment and laughter, of course, fuelled in part by the alcohol-bearing hip-flasks carried by many, but with it a thread of steely intent runs. The percussive shaking of collection buckets also reminds you of another part to all this, as money is collected for local charities. Lewes, for all its fiery moments, has a long history of philanthropy and social responsibility, continued today.

The radiance from the flames, passing just above the faces of those in the first tier of pavement dwellers, is intense and some flinch from the extremes of heat and the cold November air, eyes smarting and watering in the smoke. Discarded torches, burning too far down for comfort, or expended, form little bonfires in the gutters.

Some flaming stakes are mounted on larger shields and emblems, the proud Roman-like standards bearing the initials, mottoes and traditional artwork of each society. Even these are held as sacred, not to be toyed with or crossed. The town has not yet forgotten the furore stirred recently when one society commissioned a new banner based on a famous Bonfire painting already used by another and held as their traditional mascot alone. Tonight a truce is in place, the new banner left at home for this year, though its very existence leaves the fuse alight on a brooding controversy which threatened the unity of the Bonfire Council and the Grand Procession itself. The struggle for the purity, heart and soul of Bonfire continues.

But there, held high on stakes or carts, are images of the very character whose fate gave birth to all this - Guido

Fawkes, stovepipe-hatted, bearded, moustached, an archetypal identikit figure of men from Jamesian times, an unfortunate stooge for a wider conspiracy. He rides high above the crowds, paraded in everlasting shame for attempting to wrong England's Monarchy and Parliament. Tonight he will burn for attempting to change a nation's mind by force. In alternative dimensions he could be Protestant, Baptist, Jesuit, Muslim, Hindu, Buddhist, Jew, but here he is Catholic, sacrificed as a symbol of one who fought intolerance with intolerance, a terrorist of older times. Several 'Guys', some huge, reaching to the lamp posts, some of more human proportions pass by. He will be burnt - or more accurately, exploded with ridiculous, but amusing force - many times tonight; a perhaps more humane fate than that which met

the real Guido and his fellow conspirators, hung until nearly dead, but not dead enough not to be able to appreciate the agony and terror of having their own intestines and internal organs forcibly ripped from their bodies and sported in front of them. Understandably, this small historical detail is forgotten in the spirit of com-memoration and celebration. Some of the societies (most famously Cliffe) go one further and actually explode Pope Paul V too, an *increased* practice among them in recent times; NO POPERY banners have begun to creep back in defiance since attempts by some local figures to end the tradition.

All this takes place to a backdrop of pounding, blood-raising beats, chime bars and fanfares from a myriad of marching bands and majorettes, the clip-clop of clogs from Morris Men and walloping explosions from rookies hazardously cast amongst the feet of the marchers or into the open fires of rattling ember carts. Your chosen High

Street location determines the intensity of the resulting con-cussion, the narrower stretches accentuating the sound and dulling the hearing for minutes afterwards. For the sensitive, cotton wool is a prime requisite for the Fifth. One learns to watch for Bonfire Boys or youths with tiny orange glows  and walk the other way. When those glows go bang in a twitten or enclosed space, the eardrums know about it.

One year, a particularly lethal pyrotechnic went off with all the force of a small bomb in the skylight-covered passage of the old Market Tower, just off the War Memorial. The glass roof shattered instantly, raining fragments. A blast shockwave was felt by those lining the street outside. Though an extreme case, those new to the unexpected surprises thrown by Lewes Bonfire can find it a disturbing experience. Attractive portable tableaux ignited from time to time and Bonfire Boys bearing radiant flares aloft, illuminating faces with their crimson glow, are tolerable, but many are not ready for the detonation of Chinese Crackers, long chains of paper-bound charges lit without warning during processions. They go off like Gatling guns in rapid fire, showering white flakes. These are the kind of surprises which in turn can spark letters of rebuke in the local press, largely from outsiders to the town, protesting of resultant family traumas. Visitors are not always prepared for the hardiness of the celebrations, expecting nothing more than a jolly carnival they and their

children can roam freely around. But the Fifth in Lewes is much, much more than a jolly carnival and brings risks for the unwary. Such outrage from newcomers merely reinforces the view of some that spectators from afar should stay away.

20:37   Squeeze

Suddenly the Grand Procession is thinning and surging down behind the final torches is a huge black mass of humanity in pursuit. This is where one must decide to retreat to one of the side passages - almost impossible this year thanks to the police - or go with the tide of bodies. Standing still is not an option. Computer studies of mass-movement shows that sticking to the sides is best for continuing motion, avoiding the inevitable plug at the centre of a flow. From our traditional position at Shelley's Hotel, we would always ensure contact with a wall on one side and head east towards the centre of the town.

The momentum of the crowd propels you almost effortlessly but breaking out of this auto-pilot is not always easy. At the chest-crushing squeeze of the 'bottleneck' by the old West Gate boundary, we would escape to the dark cobbles of Keere Street where, despite acquiring sympathy for the poor horses allegedly driven at full pelt down this steep drop for a bet by a reckless George IV long ago, one could at least breathe again. Not this year though. A metal gate bars the way and the High Street is the only funnel. There were wry smiles in the masses, no doubt, from some inching past Bull House, once home to Thomas Paine in the 1700's, another outspoken freedom fighter of years past. For him even Lewes was too tame and his writings would take him across the Atlantic to play his part in the

New World's own struggles for liberty. He wouldn't think much of the street barriers.

The main procession is a useful starting point for the guideless brave witnessing the sights for the first time with no idea of what's going on. It is a massively disorientating experience to enter the proceedings partway through the evening not knowing who to follow, where to go or when anything takes place. Where you wind up - a firesite, nine times out of ten - usually depends on which crowd you follow. The Grand provides an anchor for the night, always leading somewhere useful in the end even if it's only to one of the myriad burger bars now clustered against their will in the car park behind the Friars Walk law courts. Once they lined every available piece of grass and kerb across the town, bequeathing a legacy of litter and tyre-marks without recourse or recompense to anyone, but more recent legislation has streamlined them too and licenses and restrictions are enforced.

Astonishingly, some attempt to leave Lewes after the Grand. In 1997, rail operators were caught out at this point as thousands of drenched spectators gave up the fight against the malicious elements and themselves poured down towards the station, blocking the bridge from Lansdown Place, only to find no special trains due until much later. To retreat so early is to miss the climax of the Fifth which comes in the next hour and, rain or no rain, deserves attendance and commitment. True devotees soldier on.

20:59   Effigies

Some are belting pell-mell to catch one of the most impressive scenes of the night - though still not yet the climax. Whichever society they ultimately support at the firesites, many stop off first between School Hill and Cliffe Bridge to await Cliffe's main procession. Several societies parade impressive tableaux through the town but many await the unveiling of Cliffe's latest towering effigy of devastating satire with particular relish. It can be a sight never forgotten.

The pedestrianisation of Cliffe High Street's western end hasn't stopped the procession passing through each year. Now the town square it has become is packed with onlookers, impatient to see what famous personality, politician or global situation has offended the sensibilities of the Society enough to be dragged through the street - and, figuratively, through the mud. Like all societies' set-pieces, known only to the chosen few, the effigy's identity is a deadly secret which would only be broken by someone foolish enough to risk total ostracisation from the local community. It happened to Cliffe once a long time ago, but only a truly blackened soul would wish to spoil the fun again.

Impatience at the wait breeds more of the mischief which history records has always been a part of Bonfire, and youthful shenanigans can spark at this point. I remember clearly a sky rocket being lit flat to the ground a few years back and watching it part the crowds like a bow-wave as it drove a fiery course across the paving before exploding in an enclosed shop front. (Wise

retailers block their letterboxes.) Such misdemeanours are tame compared with japes of yore; years ago 'Lewes rousers', deadly home-made explosives which made the devices of today seem impotent, were openly cast into crowds by marchers themselves before their use was outlawed. Even so, the rookies which regularly rock the precinct tonight still manage to set off - as always - an irritating chorus of burglar alarms which ring themselves stupid for the rest of the night.

But the tell-tale waft of bandsmen sounds in the air alerts ears to the imminent arrival of spectacle and all such distractions cease. With faces set even harder than some of those seen in the Grand, Cliffe takes the business of marching seriously and the proliferation of torch-bearing warriors in the shape of Vikings, Cavaliers and Roundheads intensifies the grimmer but captivating atmosphere.

Banners carried beneath those already stretched across the narrow street remember the Lewes martyrs, the discovery of the Gunpowder Plot and the arrival on our shores of the one-time saviour of English Protestant rule, William of Orange, on another November 5th in 1688. In this commemoration one can see more clearly the link some draw between Lewes Bonfire and the 'marching season' in parts of Northern Ireland. What connections remain are largely of historical value rather than contemporary, although the Reverend Ian Paisley - to the societies' disapproval - did once turn up to witness the proceedings and has preached in the town at the old Jireh chapel, where a Bonfire service, somewhat controversially, is still held each year.

Guy Fawkes, of course, and a snarling figure of Pope Paul V are carried to their doom, chaperoned by the inevitable blazing letters 'NO POPERY'. Other effigies of

more local significance usually bob by; the 'Enemies of Bonfire', large firework-packed papier-mâché severed heads on pikes portraying authority or community figures who may have crossed the Society in the last twelve months. Councillors, MPs, even priests, have all found their images raised and bleeding above the crowds on the Fifth.

This year banner-squabbling Bonfire Boys themselves are targeted. No-one is too sacred to be an Enemy.

But here is what many have come to see, its upper portion peering over the hump of Cliffe Bridge before dramatically swinging into full view. A huge, brilliantly executed and lavishly painted pyrotechnic sculpture, dragged on wheels by sweating Bonfire Boys and Girls, looms high over the crowds through which laughter and

applause ripple. This year, America's President Clinton and his clandestine physical pleasures are lampooned in an obscene tribute of phallic Cruise missiles, Viagra, Bill as Captain America and hilarious slogans unfit to print. Past works of art still linger in the memory... the BSE crisis, John Major... you can guess many of them but there's always a twist of genius and

humour in their execution and this year is no exception. Again, Lewes shows its righteous anger at those who abuse positions of power for their own ends. It almost seems a shame to explode these marvels but explode they must to drive their point home. Incredible to think that less than a century ago such a tableau would have been *set off* at this point, instead of passing to the safer outskirts of the town,

as the societies had their firesites and displays in the streets as a matter of routine.

Cliffe's procession passes into Eastgate Street and returns to School Hill via

Albion Street, providing a breathtaking view as the effigies and marchers descend and pass into Friars Walk, onwards to their display. People cling perilously to lamp posts and shin up trees to savour the moment.

Throughout the whole of Lewes, all the societies and their guests from the provinces have extricated themselves from the Grand and regroup to make their different ways to the flaming pyres awaiting their arrival for the climax of the evening to begin. The more central parts of the town are served by Waterloo at Malling Brooks, Commercial Square at Landport and South Street at the old railway land by the Ouse. The southern outskirts are the domain of Cliffe at Ham Lane (replacing their old outgrown site of Malling Hill) and, north-west, furthest out of all, Borough at the top of Nevill Road. No other town in the world has as many bonfires in one night across such a relatively small area. The panorama of Lewes is splattered with resplendent beacons.

Now one must decide. Here, loyalties are tested. As each society processes to their firesite, militant Lewesians will pursue their traditional allegiance but more casual spectators must gamble as to which to follow and which will provide the loudest and most glorious dance of fireworks.
Where indecision strikes, the herd instinct soon takes over and some allow their choice to be determined by the general direction of the most human activity and are led accordingly. Any continuing inertia is soon overcome by heading for the nearest gleam of fire over the rooftops, although some eventually find their way barred by those societies which now only admit bearers of tickets sold in the run-up to the Fifth, a recent trend.

21:33   Conflagration

At each sacred site of tradition or modern equivalent of convenience, huge stacks of flame burn high into the cold night sky and masses of huddled bodies push as  close as they can without scorching. The conflagrations are so hot you almost can't bear to turn your face towards them, yet the lure against the icy air outside is too great. Life begins to flow again through frozen cheeks. The bonfires have been piled with wood and various flammable debris collected by the societies for weeks. In these times of pathological delinquency, round the clock watches guard against the plague of firebugs which struck Lewes a few years back, causing the pyres to burn before their time.

Here, the pagan connections with Bonfire, the echoes of festivals and rituals of old, which will strike home harder the following day for me, are clear to see. Fire illuminating the darkness, the primal allure for the people gathered around it in their hundreds, seeking warmth but also held spellbound by each leap and lick of the flames... Just for a few minutes you realise some human fascinations haven't changed very much. In 1997, an unexpected gift from the sheets of water which turned many of the firesites into paddling pools was the huge rippling mirror created like a mirage on the ground, doubling the luminosity of the blazes.

21:42   Pyrotechnics

Now figures begin to drift outwards to the darker boundaries of the field where ropes enclose the danger zone. Here, tableaux and effigies are erected, waiting in ominous silence, ready to burst forth at the touch of a flame or the pulse of an electronic charge.

People wait too. Delays can hold up processions and schedules can never be relied on at this point. This can be the most uncomfortable part of the Fifth. By now, things which have so far escaped attention through the constant momentum of the evening begin to edge their way into consciousness. A pause of stillness means aching feet and lowering body temperatures are revealed and intensified. It's at this point also, that you begin to wish you'd gone to the loo when you last had the chance. But rookies still bang and attenders intent on providing their own amusement keep the crowds occupied by letting off rockets, pretty for now but soon to be eclipsed by spangled detonations in another league altogether.

In five separate locations in one town the same scenario is being played out. The procession finally arrives and any extra tableaux brought with it are dragged into place. Just to one side of the enclosed area stands what looks for all the world like a boxing ring. Onto this platform of planks and scaffolding the 'clergy' clamber, the hierarchy of the societies, ready to address the waiting crowds in what will be little more than an unintelligible shout to all but those who swarm closely around.

Astonishingly, as the mock bishops and priests, replete with mitres and crooks, bark their 'sermon' at the masses, a hail of rookies is thrown, exploding just inches away from their faces. Newcomers expecting the police to be called wonder what on earth is going on. But this is tradition. The Gatling-gun crackers ignite beneath the platform as a further rain of detonations fly through the air. Cassocks are often burnt and blackened but projectiles (including,

unbelievably, the occasional sky rocket aimed horizontally) that get too near can provoke a heated and sometimes profane verbal riposte in a manner most unbecoming of a cleric. Either plugs must be employed or a few hearing problems may be coming these people's way in later life. It may be no accident that at one site, in real life, one of those wearing the garb is a fire officer and another an ambulanceman... In some respects this is the most priceless moment of Bonfire, being both hilarious and wondrous that such a treacherous sanctioned activity could develop. Perhaps it is the enduring legacy of some kind of general revenge wish on the authority figures of *all* clerics, no matter what denomination.

Despite the potentially deadly hail, somehow the preacher gets through a garbled rant, usually on modern local issues and the need to maintain traditions which remember the important symbolism of the Gunpowder Plot. Some of the infamous 'Bonfire Prayers' may be recited. Whatever else is swept away on the breeze or buried in the chatter of the increasingly restless crowds (suspecting they are actually being kept on hold deliberately to build the tension), one line always stands out, bellowed forth at the fullest volume the speaker can muster: "WHAT SHALL WE DO WITH HIM..?" Most know the answer, which builds in volume across the field on each ritual repetition: "BURN HIM!" It seems rather sick when looked at in the cold light of day, a kind of mob rule culture, but from such origins part of Bonfire comes down to us. Their wishes are finally answered by the ignition of the first set-piece, usually Guy himself, who begins his fiery destruction.

Silver fountains spring from his head, beginning a routine which will be followed by most tableaux tonight; the pretty stuff first, emphasis on sparkly colours, building to the more entertaining balletic twisting, whistling and screaming ballistics. And then, of course, the fuses move on to

the bangs, the last of which, seemingly placed to demolish what may remain, is always the deepest, a rich, low bass boom which vibrates the chest and flaps the trousers. Each set piece goes up with ever-increasing power and longevity. In-between, rockets and missiles punch the sky with beautiful shapes and hues. These tend to be the most successful of the night's array; everyone can see them. Those of shorter stature are spared the peering over of heads, shoulders, and in 1997, to much annoyance, umbrellas. (Yet one advantage the umbrellas brought was the added protection from debris falling from the sky. I remember one year at Waterloo watching a dying rocket plummet straight into the ground about ten feet away, miraculously seeking the gap between packs of shocked onlookers.)

The joy of fireworks in Lewes, however, is the cacophony of sonic exchanges between each firesite which fly across the town. Its topography and terrain, unevenly surrounded by broken walls of downland,

ensures plenty of *echo*. For every explosive crack, a succession of aftershocks ring around the hills and buildings like quadraphonic ricochets. The effect is exhilarating and ecstatic, building to a crescendo as each display peaks, *seen* as well as heard from whichever firesite you choose by the telltale glow, the blossoming bursts above the chimneys and the time-delayed decibels. It's hard not to look over your shoulder while watching your own chosen society's efforts to see how the competition is shaping up.

But the very best place from which to view *all* of this is Chapel Hill, perched above the massive chalk cliff faces to the east of the town. And here is where I choose to be in 1998, for the first time, in an effort to witness in one night the totality of the Lewes Bonfire experience.

I am amazed at how many people are here, crawling like ants up this narrow and very steep lane which rises from South Street and ascends the Downs to provide one of the most stunning views of Lewes. Gazing westwards the whole town is spread before you, slightly to the right, while the Ouse snakes its way below and outwards to the south. The streets of my home town twinkle and glitter, a jewelled toy, model-like at this height. Every few seconds sky rockets streak out from anywhere across the sea of rooftops.

A sheer drop lies below, yet folk are perilously settled near the lip of the chalk cliffs to absorb the awe-inspiring view. For all the beauty of Chapel Hill, there is danger. In 1836, a huge block of snow fell from here to crush dwellings below, killing as it went. In recent years a youth fell to his death in strange occult-linked circumstances. Naturally, the national newspapers salaciously ran features on Lewes as a hotbed of Satanism and perversion, dragging in Bonfire connections and ideas of religious intolerance as it went. Whilst unconnected, the local fuss caused by failed opposition to the opening of an occult bookshop in the town all helped add to the media glee. It was an easy story to blow out of proportion, tarring a whole community with the same brush. What centre of population doesn't have its darker side? Lewes is certainly a mysterious place with more to it than meets the eye, but linking Bonfire with Satanism is like coupling the Conservative Club with Nazis.

Tonight though, such dark controversies are of no

concern to those lining Chapel Hill. Unfolding beneath is a unique vision, a settlement bathed in fire and wreathed with smoke. Directly west, South Street's display is in  progress, to the south, Cliffe. Commercial Square and Waterloo are harder to see from here but their luminescence is unmistakable, and there, north-west, not far from the site of the Battle of Lewes, long, long ago, Borough's fire burns high on the horizon. There's a satisfying cyclical twist to the fact that the Battle of 1264 in its own small way paved the future for the very Parliamentary system delivered from Gunpowder Treason, commemorated here. Meanwhile, a few hundred feet to the north, on our opposing hill where Chapel Hill becomes Cuilfail, the martyrs' needle shines brightly, reminding all of one of this night's higher purposes.

Those crawling black shapes on the upper slopes are letting fireworks off above the heads of those on the cliff edge. Rockets almost graze our scalps as they head out to fall far down to the roof tiles beneath and at  every new pyrotechnic screech, we instinctively duck, lest our hair be parted. In a similar vein, being so high, the rockets soaring up from South Street's display are almost at eye-level and what one usually looks up at is practically around us, enlivening yet oddly disturbing, giving just a tiny inkling of what it must be like in a battle zone. The thought soon passes and as Lewes erupts below into orgasms of light and sound all one can do is marvel at this breathtaking and unforgettable sight.

With the fireworks spent, a river of fire streams below from the Cliffe site into town via the railway land as torch bearers make their way back to the streets for the final processions. The crowds atop Chapel Hill disperse and descend to meet them, stopping briefly to witness Waterloo's colourful sky-bursts, the last tonight due to technical delays, we discover later. I chance a final view across the extraordinary vista. I will return here tomorrow.

23:11   Desolation

At the firesites, the tableaux and effigies are now little more than ashen rubble, blown to the four winds, although occasionally a curious onlooker can be surprised by the sudden late ignition of a lone charge. A thinning ring of silhouettes surround the dying fires, mesmerised by magical licks of purple and green deep inside the glowing embers which can smoulder for days or even weeks to come.

The last processions of the evening are being made as societies return to their street headquarters, and die-hards, far fewer now as a large majority make their way to the station or set out on long treks to cars left far outside the town, proceed wearily but happily to catch up with them for the final Bonfire Prayers.

It's at this point that the scale of what has happened here tonight really hits you. Walking up the High Street reveals a post-holocaust sea of litter, smoking fragments and other fallout from intense human habitation, cans, cigarettes, crushed onions fallen from hot dogs, alcoholic vomit... it's all here. Yet there's something exhilarating about carving your way through all this, watching ambulances and fire tenders crawl slowly around, flickering blue illuminating the mathematical tiles of old Lewes, policemen casting beady eyes on potential troublemakers, drink-provoked teenage dramas breaking out... There is a price to pay for the freedom of the streets, but the joy of strolling the tarmac of a traffic-free town *en-masse* is a valuable and strangely empowering experience. For one night, people are the priority and a population has spoken out in a way denied to most. The increasing authoritarian restrictions are an irritation, but one remembers that in some countries even small such expressions would be arrestable heresy. Tonight, liberty has been asserted and used where - and while - it can be.

Burger and tea bars scrape the last blackened scraps into soggy bread for the really hungry before packing up and the first cars inadvisably begin to inch their way past trudging bodies who must now decide whether to head home or go the last leg for the final marvel of the evening.

23:46   Prayers

Small street fires have sprung up in roads at society headquarters where cars usually dominate, the last bastions of the old pre-streamlining days, and sweaty, grimy, costumed or bestriped figures prepare to end the celebrations. Now an intimacy can be attained. The thousands of visitors from colonies and counties abroad have gone and the indigenous people of Lewes are left to their own devices. This is their time alone.

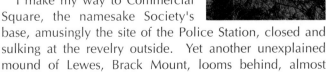

I make my way to Commercial Square, the namesake Society's base, amusingly the site of the Police Station, closed and sulking at the revelry outside. Yet another unexplained mound of Lewes, Brack Mount, looms behind, almost unseen and unnoticed. Packed into this space, Society members and Lewesians from the locale gather for the last blow-out before reality begins to set in again.

 An advantage of this site is the balcony created by Mount Pleasant, a rise of houses on the south side of the square. The ruling 'clergy' ascend the steps bearing the flaming crosses now so familiar this night. Expectation rises in the figures packed below and the counterfeit bishop makes another traditional sermon to his people from this dramatic pulpit. A powerful presence, he rails against those who have offended. The police messages which rudely broke into the remembrance ritual at the monument are blasted, Society members who don't pull their weight are cautioned and threatened with outcast... and, of course, the spark behind all this is commemorated - the Gunpowder Plot. The crowd begin a low murmur which quickly rises in volume to a chant that wouldn't disgrace a football terrace. These are the Bonfire Prayers. Here, everyone knows the words, clear at last from the garbles masked by wind and spectators at the firesite earlier. Heretical, even nasty, they retain a strange power...

"Remember, remember, the Fifth of November..."

Guy Fawkes is catch'd, the pope chokes and becomes a blazing star... Old prejudices die hard but there's little malice in the hearts of the reciters. Again, this is tradition, living history. The Bonfire Boys intend indeed that it should never be forgot. There's little to show that in Lewes, at least, it ever will be - if left unrepressed.

A minor scuffle breaks out as a bystander, worse the wear for drink, unwisely attempts to push his way past the clerics, who man-handle him back down again. Later his head will break plate glass during police attempts to subdue him. By and large though, the revellers are good-natured and sing along as the band strikes up *Sussex by the Sea*, another local anthem of old, although one which is slowly fading - far fewer seem to know the words. Its patriotic lyrics and pomp are from a bygone age when people were proud of where they came from and maintained some kind of self-respect. Lewes has done better than most in retaining these roots but self-respect in society is on the slide. If all Bonfire achieves is to keep up some kind of pride against the worst efforts of some, it is worth preserving for this alone.

Similar scenes are being replicated around Lewes. As the official deliberations close, impromptu dances and even firewalks break out around the embers and Lewesians begin their weary but satisfied strolls homeward at last. Even those in costume are giving up now, leaving only the hardcore, some of whom drift down to join their brothers and sisters at Cliffe, society loyalties now blurred. Firewalking inevitably breeds scars and burns but has old origins and remains the choice of those left to themselves with cans and hip-flasks, communing long into the night. Lewes at last falls into a dreamy sleepful state, an afterglow.

00:37   Home

Already the Fifth is another day and I walk through the now almost quiet neon-lit roads to find my car. Other homegoers pass by, but become increasingly rare sightings. Even now, still the odd explosive pop echoes through the cold damp air, filled with a smoggy, smoky mist. It's time to go home, to conformity and responsibility.

As a child, long before I ever knew the evening went on so long in other parts of the town, I always found it hard to accept that Bonfire Night was over. I would sleep with the curtains open just in case there was one more sparkle to catch. Sometimes I would strike lucky, but most often the fight against heavy eyes would be lost and I would fall into content, exhausted oblivion where the events of the night would replay over and over again in sleep's realm of imagination. At weekends, I would be up the next morning to search our local roads and gardens for dead rockets fallen mysteriously from the sky. In a counterpart feeling to the excitement at an unlit firework's potential, there was always a sad, strange curiosity about discovering something now inert which was once so alive and mobile, which had travelled far higher than I could ever jump, up to the clouds it seemed. To find such a merrily decorated tube cold, empty and abandoned, perhaps lined with morning frost or dew, provoked an odd hollow feeling in the stomach, a kind of sweet pain at something beautiful passed.

Many feel something similar in Lewes on the sixth of November. Yet, for me, the morning also brings revelation and clarity...

Epilogue: November The Sixth

9:32   Contemplation

Returning to Lewes the morning after Bonfire is like trying to piece together the fragments of a lost dream. The crack team of dawn street cleaners do their work well. All that remains of last night's extraordinary events are faint traces, the odd torch ember maybe, a dead rocket missed in the gutter... It's hard to believe the events of just hours before really happened. Life has returned to normal and only the activity of joiners removing planks from windows, black patches in the road where fires burned and a pervading, but nostalgic hint of kerosene in the clear morning air reminds you that here, magic took place, irreplaceable and unique. I decide to return to Chapel Hill to contemplate thoughts which have been accumulating since yesterday, kept to the periphery until now by the wonderful distractions of the celebrations themselves.

There my home town lies before me, an even more astonishing sight than the glittering shadowland of last night, glowing softly in the sun's autumnal gold, the river a band of light running through its heart. In daylight the encompassing landscape is revealed and Lewes is placed into context. The smooth and feminine curves of the Kingston Ridge hills lie to the south west, the far blue of the sea peering in-between before Firle Beacon rises to the south east, while the tree-dotted agricultural plains of the Sussex Weald fade to the north. And there, at the centre of all this, a soft arm of downland offers Lewes before me, descending to the valley overlooked by this escarpment.

A presenter in a recent television documentary, passing through Lewes as she walked the South Downs Way, remarked on how glad she was to leave its "claustrophobic" atmosphere and small-town politics. How could she know anything of anywhere from a stay of no more than a few hours? But at least she felt a distinctive energy of some kind. It's not a place for the bland or faint-hearted and like an electric current anything which interacts with it must tune into its wavelength for a smooth ride. Lewes - and other towns with a strong presence - sorts out for itself those who will inhabit it. Some fear this presence; I have heard people from outside comment on the strong 'negative' feelings which emanate from the area with all its strange Bonfire goings-on and (supposed) religious animosity. Ultimately, Lewes reflects back and amplifies what you take in with you, be it fear or delight. It is a place of incredible power and once roots are put down few choose to extricate them. Up here, I realise that for me and others I know, Lewes is the centre of the Universe, a source of joy and a living memory of something much deeper than just a site of dwelling. Sometimes I wonder why.

Looking west from Chapel Hill, the eye is naturally drawn to the highest point of the town; the castle. A symbol of authority and a watchtower in ages past, its remains perch on a domed platform of earth and greenery, the lord of all it surveys. It is ironic that a town so dominated by such a symbol, constructed as much to oppress as to defend, has also come to represent the struggle for freedom of expression.

It has long been assumed by historians that the castle's supporting mound was merely the construction of labouring Normans. But turning just a little to the north, a conundrum lies: another mound, slightly smaller yet still substantial, with only minimal signs of structures or habitation. Surrounded now by the roads of Castle Banks and the telling names Mount Pleasant and Mount Place, eaten into on one side by what is now the *Lewes Arms* pub, Brack Mount sits, ambiguous, unexplained and virtually ignored by eyes trained in the received wisdom that all it represents is a dump of waste or an aborted phase of the castle's construction. Look again. And then compare the virtually identical castle mound.

Then look further south to the spiralled Tump of another appropriate street name, Mountfield Road, Christianised each Easter, hidden by trees on one side, margined by a bowling green and dwarfed by a football club on another. Again, it remains an unexplained enigma, up to now considered an Elizabethan garden folly or perhaps a tip of dried slurry from the old vanished salt flats known as 'The Dripping Pan'.

In my mind I strip away the roads and houses and travel backwards in time. Recent scrutiny of archaeological findings made in and around the two central mounds over the last two centuries suggest strongly that we can permit ourselves to travel much further back than most historians have previously allowed, back before the Normans, back even before the Saxon settlers who set up what would become the Lewes of today. Buildings vanish, tarmac unravels, trees begin to cover empty spaces and, perhaps even, the shining sea rolls back over the fields from Newhaven and onwards to the estuary shores of what will one day be Southover. We stand 2000 or so years in the past. Of that which has vanished from our sight, three landmarks remain - and others have joined them. Brack Mount and the castle mound, perhaps now a little smaller and minus its adorning structure, stand out proud from their downland slope while the Tump, in this vision of a possible past, guards the south, looking out across the water. But keeping the first two company are four further mounds. On what will be the yard of St John sub Castro church, two similar-looking edifices mark the northern boundary, while another two fill the gap between Brack Mount, one on the adjoining corner of the future Abinger Place and another on the site of *The Elephant and Castle.*

There is modern evidence to show that even until the late 18th century these extra mounds, now lost to us by urbanisation, were still in existence. Historical documents of the time make reference to them, if obscurely, and some old maps mark them. An illustration of one and a drawing of Lewes sketched *from the top* of another have come down to us. The theories are only just breaking surface to inevitable controversy, but increasingly persuasive evidence suggests that Lewes was built around a series of ancient ritual burial mounds, perhaps in the late Bronze Age, but more probably Iron Age or early Roman. What has been taken as a Norman foundation for the castle was probably *already there* long before King William arrived on the shores of Sussex and was simply appropriated and augmented for its ideal properties. The Tump may have a separate origin, shaped differently to its sisters but in a manner virtually identical to that of Wiltshire's mysterious Silbury Hill and placed south of the main complex. Like Silbury's connections with nearby Avebury, the Tump appears to be placed in distinct alignments with other ancient landmarks; from it the first glow of the Midsummer sunrise shines above the barrows of Cliffe Hill.

Now, perhaps, the very name *Lewes* begins to explain itself more clearly, long suspected to have derived from the Old English *hlaewas*, which means mounds or hills, whatever other influences may have shaped the word (some also see links with the sub-Roman-Brittanic word *lechwedd*, meaning slope). A Sussex variation on *hlaewas*, though, is telling: *hlaew* and *hlaw* specifically refer to *artificially* constructed mounds or tumuli. Place names don't come about by accident. They have a long ancestry which can take us back to their foundations. It seems that the earliest settlers of this site may have defined it by giving it the name of the very structures which possibly shaped its history in more ways than one.

Silbury Hill has revealed no burial remains through excavation nor has the similar Tump; their origin and purpose remain a mystery. The castle and Brack mounds, however, have given up pottery, ritual bones of fowl and from the latter, even a complete human skeleton in years past. Another burial site was identified in the last century at the Western Road reservoir and there are suggestions that a standing stone once sat where the All Saints Centre is today. From this, it is easy to visualise the conical towers adorning the final slopes of this smooth downland promontory as a large and very important ritual cemetery complex - and perhaps more - in its day, which, unlike the mighty stones and embankments of Avebury and Stonehenge, have been long forgotten to the point that Lewes has lost sight of its own true heritage. Yet echoes from that long distant past still reach us - through tradition. Standing looking over this place I love, I try to extend the scope of my journey back through time, to picture the people who first chose this place for sacredness and marked it so solemnly. But here, the mind meets an impenetrable wall. How can 2000 years be bridged, to know people as alien to us today as we will be to our descendants two millennia hence? Their thoughts, their lives and their intentions will forever be a mystery to us - but perhaps some of their rituals remain.

It has long been recognised that the Bonfire traditions of today hold parallels to certain pagan ways descending from the November Samhain celebration and other festivals of fire. The lighting of beacons across the country to communicate events of significance was already long established before Guy Fawkes and his conspirators met their unfortunate fate. When the edicts decreeing fire and rejoicing to mark King and Parliament's deliverance from the Gunpowder Plot were made, there must have been a measure of calculation that this would take and shape old practices in much the same way most Christian feast days were superimposed over existing rites. But the Bonfire celebrations, especially those of Lewes (which also recall its old rowdy St Pancras day processions in the 1300's), have as much in common with the fire festivals of quite another season - Midsummer.

Perusing centuries-old accounts of this most important of festivities is revealing. Street fires, costumed torch processions, pageantry, running across embers, many of the trappings familiar to Lewesians today, all are there. Flaming wheels would even be rolled down hills in divination to determine the outcome of the harvest... Only relatively recently was the tradition of rolling flaming tar barrels down the hilly streets of Lewes reshaped into less hazardous forms. Midsummer has always been a most sacred time, the point of the year where the sun stops in the sky before its slow descent into the long months of cold and strife. Here, entreaties for plenty in the imminent reaping and appeasement of the gods for merciful treatment in the dark season were essential for generations convinced their destinies were held in the hands of greater beings. Though attempts to Christianise the celebrations developed, the threatening influence of the old gods remained too strong and, quietly, official suppression had to weaken Midsummer's hold on the festival year. Whether as a clandestine attempt to preserve pagan ways or a resigned effort from authorities to translate them into new contexts, slowly elements from the Midsummer celebrations were absorbed into other feast days. November the Fifth was an ideal place for many of them to escape to under a new guise.

The feast of St John the Baptist on June 24th (closely followed by that of St Peter and St Paul on the 28th) was

that chosen by the church to deliberately eclipse Midsummer, much as Christmas obliterated its counterpart, Midwinter. Is it coincidence that Lewes has had a long history of churches by the name of St John - a surprisingly uncommon English dedication - currently embodied in St John the Baptist at Southover and St John sub Castro, site of two burial mounds now removed? In times now unreachable, this town may once have been a thriving cathedral to gods now departed, perhaps a Midsummer gathering point for the devout of long-vanished generations. The Midsummer light rising over the Cliffe barrows provides another clue that it may have been.

It seems that what has been handed down to us to flower on the Fifth may be a form of worship and commemoration that has survived the twists and turns of plagues, famines, wars, superimposed meaning and outright suppression for many centuries. Despite pauses in its continuity, with near-fades into obscurity at times, the rituals embodied in the Lewes Bonfire celebrations have always revived and returned, like a thread that cannot be broken. It is a line which may stretch back, however thinly, to those unreachable souls who first colonised this beautiful corner of the world.

What drew them here in the first place, beyond its natural beauty, to construct their feats of ceremonial soil engineering? There are those who believe the Earth is laced with a network of natural energy, piezoelectric fields generated by underground quartz and running water. Not quite leys, which in truth are alignments in the landscape, those like dowsers who study these energy lines and strive to prove their existence hold that they fluctuate in width and intensity, crossing at some points like huge strands in a web. These areas are often marked by ancient structures. Did earlier civilisations instinctively recognise and mark these connections in the energy network, like healers and acupuncturists seek active places in the body's 'meridian lines'? Were stone temples, mounds and barrows built to capture and hold this energy as well as commemorate the dead and provide celestial observatories? Many believe so. If any truth resides in these ideas then Lewes must be strong indeed in such energies, a major junction made visible by the mound builders. If this source can be drawn on and shapes the mindset of those that live upon its active centres, as speculation suggests, then maybe we have another answer of sorts which solves an age old question regarding Bonfire: 'Why Lewes?'. Perhaps it sits on a natural circuit which intensifies and transforms anything generated within its influence. It is certainly hard to be passive in Lewes. Extremes of views and open expression are stirred easily.

A journey back in time... Gazing out across the Ouse valley from the castle mound to Brack Mount and its sisters. Pastel drawing by Andy Gammon.

65

The Fifth is the most glaring example of this. Though this power may have been used and abused by various authorities for their own ends throughout Bonfire's Gunpowder Plot-shaped history, Lewesians have always asserted a spin of their own and modern thinking has turned the focus of the Fifth into a fight for the general right of freedom. The religious themes may be little more than a catalyst for a more cryptic meaning, the tail end of the thread from the deep past.

There is no hotline to early times, no continuing record of where we have come from; as such it's often hard to see where we're going, to put it all into context. Only ritual and tradition carry the thread. For all the different expressions of fire ceremonies, the same basic ingredients come up time and again, like a race memory. Even long pauses in their implementation and the absence of documentation doesn't seem to cut this bond to earlier wisdom. Just folklore's word of mouth, perhaps, something in the genes or some collective imprint in the Earth picked up by successive generations? We may never know but we shouldn't be complacent that the thread won't break. At all costs, ritual and tradition must be preserved because it's all we have to link us to what we once were. For all our modern understanding of the Universe, somewhere deep within us remains the fear that we dance on the strings of superior forces which still need appeasing. And so from our subconscious needs the old expressions have continued and for Lewes, Bonfire Night is the last vestige, preserving actions with meanings, however buried, which remain available for decoding and interpretation. A few communities across Britain still remember the Fifth, but its influence is diminishing by the year and with it is leaking knowledge of our past which could one day be wiped for good. Lewes has kept up the celebrations, against all repression, modern and historical. For now its heritage is intact. It must be allowed to stay that way.

10:17   Life

It's time to leave Chapel Hill. I stand in the present once more. The sun climbs higher and the thin mist disperses, the acrid hint of smoke in the air thankfully remaining, keeping the events of last night lodged in consciousness just a little longer from a town quickly moving back into the daily routines of life. It feels good to be alive.

In the days which follow, as ever, nothing I read of this year's Bonfire celebrations manages to capture its real essence, its meaning or its *soul*. I begin to have some thoughts as to how it might be done and decide that maybe, somewhere, I should write it all down.

Appendix

READING

While writing this book, I found several sources of information particularly
helpful and I include them here for anyone who wishes to find out more
background on some of the topics covered. Bear in mind these are just a
selection of relevant titles available.

The Bonfire Celebrations

For those wanting to know more about the detailed history of the Lewes
celebrations and the Bonfire Societies, the accepted 'bible' is Jim
Etherington's *Lewes Bonfire Night* (S B Publications 1993, revised 1999)
and comes highly recommended. Following on from this, Jim produced
Bonfire (S B Publications 1997), a larger format book which shows the
activities of the societies on the Fifth in black and white photographs.

Filling in details on some of the other Sussex Bonfire Society events,
Brigid Chapman's *Night of the Fires* (S B Publications 1994) shows that
despite Lewes being the centre of attention, the active dedication of
groups out in the provinces shouldn't be neglected.

In addition, I found notes in all the Bonfire Society programmes, sold
annually in the run up to the Fifth, usefully informative. For the full story
of Guy Fawkes and the Gunpowder Plot, readers are referred to any number
of history tomes which have appeared over the years.

As Andy Freeman points out in his foreword, in the closing days of my
writing this book I was introduced to Arthur Beckett's beautifully-written
paean to the Sussex countryside *The Spirit of the Downs.* First published
in 1909, and revised and republished several times, finally by Methuen &
Co. in 1949, this lost local classic features a chapter entitled *A Southdown
Saturnalia* which records the Lewes Bonfire proceedings of the day in a
manner not dissimilar to the book you hold now, if more concisely. It is
a valuable record and an interesting comparison from another age if you
can find a copy.

Lewes

There is a plethora of Lewes books out there, covering all aspects of its
rich past, but for a compact compendium Barbara Fleming's *Lewes: Two
Thousand Years of History* (S B Publications 1994) is particularly helpful.
For the more dedicated scholar, John Houghton's *Unknown Lewes*
(Tartarus Press 1997) is an extraordinary glimpse into its previous ages as
recorded in local legal documents and includes Lambert's 1778 painting
of Lewes as seen from one of the now removed mounds in St John sub
Castro's churchyard.

Mounds and Rituals

I am hugely indebted to the work of Lewes historian John Bleach for having
brought to my attention his view that the town was constructed on the site
of a burial mound complex. His enlightening 1998 presentation at the

Lewes Festival confirmed a few of my own suspicions and helped shape the Epilogue to this book. His findings, including illustrations and diagrams, have been published as a paper in *Sussex Archaeological Collections: Vol. 135, 1997* and demand much greater attention, which I hope this book may in a small way help achieve. I should also acknowledge the contribution of Richard Coates to this paper as regards speculation on the origins of the name Lewes.

John Bleach, in turn, alerted me to the works of Ronald Hutton, whose very detailed explorations of the traditions and rituals of England in *The Stations of the Sun* (Oxford University Press 1996) and *The Rise and Fall of Merry England* (Oxford University Press 1994) are utterly indispensable for anyone wishing to understand the connections between Bonfire and other ancient fire festivals. The former, in particular, contains a most illuminating chapter on the general history of the Gunpowder Plot celebrations.

For specific information on the Mountfield Road Tump and its alignments, I found Rodney Castleden's *The Wilmington Giant* (Turnstone Press 1983, planned for reissue by S B Publications in 2000) a fascinating read with many references to this much neglected landmark of Lewes. Lastly, any-one interested in the concept of earth energy lines and more esoteric explorations might like to check out *Quest For Contact* (S B Publications 1997) by myself and Paul Bura. Moving further into related earth mystery realms, the ever-controversial crop circles which have appeared around Lewes and in Sussex are explored in my own *Fields of Mystery* (S B Publications 1996). *Vital Signs* (S B Publications 1998), also by me, tells you everything you need to know about the circle phenomenon in general.

BONFIRE SOCIETIES

Roles and duties can change frequently within the societies so rather than listing contact addresses which may date quickly, those wishing to learn more of the six Lewes Bonfire Societies (Cliffe, Commercial Square, Lewes Borough, Nevill Juvenile, South Street and Waterloo) and their activities are advised to approach the local Tourist Information Centre which always holds up-to-date records for each:

Tourist Information Centre
187 High Street
Lewes
East Sussex
BN7 2DE

Tel: 01273 483448

FIFTH CHECKLIST

For those setting out to experience the magic of Lewes Bonfire for themselves, this brief at-a-glance guide to what happens when may be helpful. As the loose chronology in this book indicates though, timings can be unreliable. For finer details, local press and Bonfire programmes should be checked.

16.30 - 17.30
Societies begin to group. Lewes is shut off to traffic.

17.30 - 18.00
First processions begin.

18.00 - 19.00
Cliffe High Street tar barrel race held. Societies process to the War Memorial for remembrance ceremonies.

19.00 - 19.40
Martyrs' setpiece lit at Cliffe Bridge. Further processions and remembrance ceremonies. Tar barrels cast into Ouse from Cliffe Bridge.

19.40 - 20.40
United Grand Procession.

20.40 - 21.30
Cliffe's main procession. Societies proceed to firesites.

21.30 - 22.30
Firework displays.

22.30 - 1.00
Final processions to Society headquarters. Bonfire Prayers. Roads reopen.

As a piece of general advice to non-Lewesians determined to attend against all local dissuasion but unused to this kind of thing, only come if a) you are prepared for a long and sometimes cold, exhausting haul, and b) are going to get into the spirit of things and *enjoy* it. Complaining because the streets are crowded, bangers keep going off everywhere and torches keep singeing your eyebrows will not win you friends and is to miss the point - expect these things. Those with sensitive ears should bring the ever-handy cotton wool with them. Anyone more sensitive than that shouldn't be there. Incidentally, this is not an event for young children (especially in pushchairs) or dogs. You've been warned.

Wear hardy and preferably waterproof footwear with extra layers of socks (firesites can be quagmires) and for heaven's sake *wrap up warmly*. Even several jumpers on very cold nights can be inadequate and if it looks remotely like rain, make sure your coat is waterproof too. Hypothermic women shivering in mini-skirts have been seen before - it's just not worth it. Throw appearances to the wind and dress practically. And don't forget to go to the loo *before* putting sixty layers on (whatever you do, do go at every sensible opportunity - you'll regret it if you get caught short later).

If in a group, choose a distinctive meeting point in case you lose each other. This is easy to do when swept up in crowds and you don't know the town. *Don't* fall for the old chestnut of saying "I'll meet you by the fire" while in the High Street - this could be any one of five separate locations around Lewes, each crammed with thousands of faces. (Incidentally, before setting off for a firesite, it might be worth asking someone whether you'll be allowed in - some societies now only admit ticket holders who have pre-booked in the weeks before the Fifth.)

Get to the town early if travelling in a car and you don't want a two mile hike in; on the other hand expect your car to get scratched, burnt and/or vandalised if you leave it too near the centre. Rail travel is probably a better bet but beware the crush of packed bodies.

Assume that you're not necessarily welcome, be ready to have aching feet, damp clothes, ringing ears and the odd burn at the other end of the night and you'll have a great time. No, really. Read this book for proof if you haven't already.

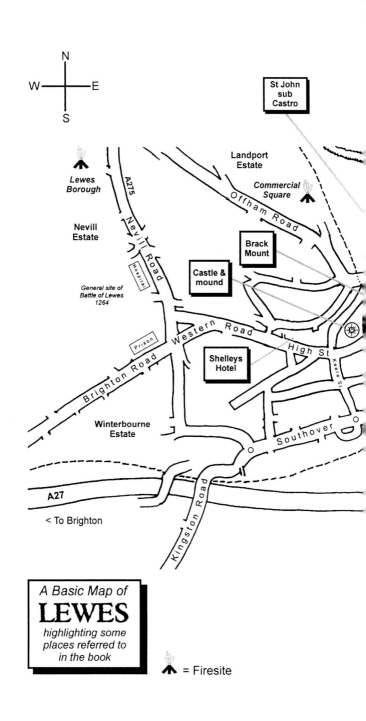

N

W —— E

S

St John
sub
Castro

Landport
Estate

Lewes
Borough

Commercial
Square

A275

Offham Road

Nevill Road

Nevill
Estate

Brack
Mount

Hospital

Castle &
mound

General site of
Battle of Lewes
1264

Western Road

High St

Prison

Keere St

Brighton Road

Shelleys
Hotel

Winterbourne
Estate

Southover

Kingston Road

A27

< To Brighton

A Basic Map of
LEWES
*highlighting some
places referred to
in the book*

🔥 = Firesite

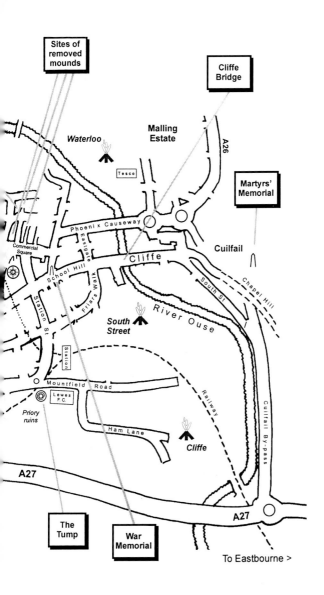

Sites of
removed
mounds

Cliffe
Bridge

Waterloo

Malling
Estate

A26

Tesco

Martyrs'
Memorial

Phoeni x Causeway

Commercial
Square

Cliffe

Cuilfail

School Hill

South St

Chapel Hill

Friars Walk

South
Street

River Ouse

Station St

Station

Mountfield   Road

Railway

Cuilfail By-pass

Lewes
F.C.

Priory
ruins

Ham Lane

Cliffe

A27

A27

To Eastbourne >

The
Tump

War
Memorial

Map by David Russell & Andy Thomas

The Author

Andy Thomas was born and bred in Lewes, East Sussex, an area he still lives in today with his wife and son.

A prolific writer and lecturer on transformational phenomena and the unexplained, Andy is also a professional musician, a founder member of the Southern Circular Research crop circle investigation team, editor of their bimonthly journal *SC* and author of three previous books; *Fields Of Mystery*, *Quest For Contact* (with Paul Bura), and *Vital Signs*.

In addition to producing his own video *Circular Sussex* in 1995, Andy has made numerous radio and TV appearances, including spots on Talk Radio UK, Channel 4's *For The Love Of...*, Meridian ITV's *The Magic & Mystery Show*, BBC 2's *Esther* and ITV's *GMTV* breakfast show.

Andy Thomas can be contacted c/o **13 Downsview Cottages, Cooksbridge, Lewes, East Sussex, BN8 4TA.**

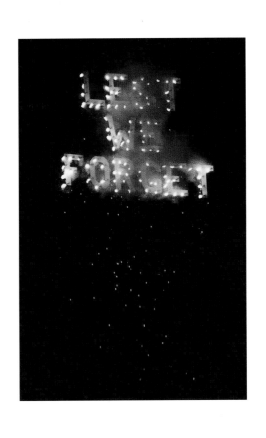